15.95

SO-BHR-846

North Chicago Public Library
2100 Argonne Dr
North Chicago, IL 60064

At Home
on the Farm

Mi casa
en la granja

Sharon Gordon

Marshall Cavendish
Benchmark
New York

This is our farm.

It is a busy place.

❖

Esta es nuestra granja.

Es un sitio de mucho trabajo.

We work hard all day long.

We start the day with a big breakfast.

---❖---

Trabajamos duro todo el día.

Empezamos el día con un gran desayuno.

Then we feed the animals.

They eat *grain*.

---❖---

Después alimentamos a los animales.

Ellos comen *grano*.

The barn is their home.

We clean it every day.

—————❖—————

El establo es su hogar.

Lo limpiamos todos los días.

We collect eggs from the chickens.

Machines pump milk from the cows.

❖

Recogemos los huevos de las gallinas.

Las máquinas ordeñan las vacas.

Our sheep have thick, soft hair called *wool*.

We cut it and sell it.

❖

El pelo grueso y suave de las ovejas se llama *lana*.

Se lo cortamos y la vendemos.

We grow *crops* on our farm.

We plant corn and wheat in the spring.

❖

Producimos *cultivos* en nuestra granja.

Sembramos maíz y trigo en la primavera.

We water the plants.

They grow tall in the summer.

❖

Regamos las plantas.

Crecen altas en el verano.

We *harvest* the crops in the fall.

We keep them in the barn.

---❖---

Cosechamos los cultivos en el otoño.

Los guardamos en el granero.

We have pets on the farm.

Our horses are fun to ride.

❖

Tenemos mascotas en
la granja.

Es divertido montar nuestros
caballos.

Our dog herds the sheep.

Our cat chases the mice.

❖

Nuestro perro pastorea las ovejas.

Nuestro gato persigue los ratones.

We go to the state fair in the summer.

The best animal wins a prize.

❖

Vamos a la feria del estado en el verano.

El mejor animal gana un premio.

In the fall, visitors come to our farm.

They always leave with a smile!

---❖---

En el otoño, vienen visitantes a nuestra granja.

¡Siempre se van con una sonrisa!

Farm Home

La casa de la granja

corn
maíz

grain
grano

harvest
cosecha

horses
caballos

28

sheep
ovejas

wool
lana

Challenge Words

crops Plants that are grown for food.

grain The seeds from wheat, corn, rice, or oats.

harvest To gather crops.

wool The thick, soft, curly hair of sheep that can be made into yarn or cloth.

Palabras avanzadas

cosechamos Recogemos los cultivos.

cultivos Las plantas que se cultivan para comer.

grano Las semillas de trigo, maíz, arroz o avena.

lana El pelo grueso, suave y crespo de la oveja que se usa para hacer hilo o tela.

Index

Índice

About the Author
Datos biográficos de la autora

Sharon Gordon has written many books for young children. She has always worked as an editor. Sharon and her husband Bruce have three children, Douglas, Katie, and Laura, and one spoiled pooch, Samantha. They live in Midland Park, New Jersey.

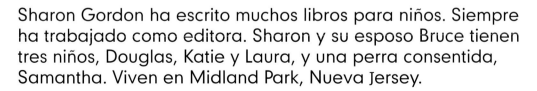

Sharon Gordon ha escrito muchos libros para niños. Siempre ha trabajado como editora. Sharon y su esposo Bruce tienen tres niños, Douglas, Katie y Laura, y una perra consentida, Samantha. Viven en Midland Park, Nueva Jersey.

31

With thanks to Nanci Vargus, Ed.D. and
Beth Walker Gambro, reading consultants

Marshall Cavendish Benchmark
99 White Plains Road
Tarrytown, New York 10591-9001
www.marshallcavendish.us

Library of Congress Cataloging-in-Publication Data

Gordon, Sharon.
[At home on the farm Spanish & English]
At home on the farm = Mi casa en la granja / Sharon Gordon. — Bilinugal ed.
p. cm. — (Bookworms. At home = Mi casa)
Includes index.
ISBN-13: 978-0-7614-2454-3 (bilingual edition)
ISBN-10: 0-7614-2454-7 (bilingual edition)
ISBN-13: 978-0-7614-2375-1 (Spanish edition)
ISBN-10: 0-7614-1958-6 (English edition)
1. Farm life—Juvenile literature. 2. Agriculture—Juvenile literature. I. Title. II. Title: Mi casa en la
granja. III. Series: Gordon, Sharon. Bookworms. At home (Spanish & English)

S519.G63418 2006b
630—dc22
2006016718

Spanish Translation and Text Composition by Victory Productions, Inc.
www.victoryprd.com

Photo Research by Anne Burns Images

Cover Photo by *Corbis*

The photographs in this book are used with permission and through the courtesy of:
Corbis: pp. 1, 15, 28 (upper l.) Richard T. Nowitz; pp. 5, 21, 28 (lower r.) Royalty Free;
pp. 7, 28 (upper r.) MacDuff Everton; p. 11 Richard Hamilton Smith; pp. 13, 29 (right) Amos
Nachoum; p. 17 Craig Aurness; pp. 19, 28 (lower l.) Philip Gould; pp. 23, 29 (left) Kevin R. Morris;
p.25 Chris Jones. *Index Stock Imagery*: p. 3 Blue Water Photo; pp. 9, 27 Frank Siteman.

Series design by Becky Terhune

Printed in Malaysia
1 3 5 6 4 2